I0172809

Chloe: A Christian Novel

Christian Youth Faith-Walkers Series

C.Orville McLeish

Published by HCP Book Publishing, 2024.

While every precaution has been taken in the preparation of this book, the publisher assumes no responsibility for errors or omissions, or for damages resulting from the use of the information contained herein.

CHLOE: A CHRISTIAN NOVEL

First edition. July 24, 2024.

Copyright © 2024 C.Orville McLeish.

ISBN: 978-1958404942

Written by C.Orville McLeish.

Also by C.Orville McLeish

Girl Unknown
Who I Am In Christ Daily Devotionals
How to Receive Your Healing
Sons of God: A Study on the Biblical Narrative of the Sons of
God
Made in God's Image: We are Partakers of God's Divine Nature
A Glorious Church: In Pursuit of the Biblical Model of
Christianity

Watch for more at https://clevelandomcleish.com/.

Table of Contents

Dedicated to all those who have been born; you are a gift to this world.

Chapter 1

The sun dipped low on the horizon, casting a warm golden glow through the dining room windows. The dinner table was meticulously set for a cozy evening meal—a crisp white tablecloth draped elegantly over the wooden table, with a centerpiece of freshly cut flowers. The soft candlelight flickered in the gentle breeze, dancing to the classical music playing softly in the background, setting a serene mood for the evening ahead. The room was filled with anticipation as Chloe went about making the final touches on setting the dinner table.

She looked magnificent and elegant in her red attire; the fabric shimmered subtly under the soft lights in the dining room. Her hair, styled in loose waves, framed her face gracefully and highlighted her features with effortless charm. A subtle hint of perfume lingered around her, a fragrance that complimented her outfit. Her eyes flickered between the clock on the wall and the front door. *It's almost time*, she thought. As she waited, she arranged the table with care, ensuring that everything was perfect for their dinner together.

With each passing moment, her heart beat a little faster, filled with a mix of excitement and longing to see him again. The very thought of him made her blush, and just then, there was a knock on the door. "Just a minute," she said, and quickly went to the mirror and touched up her hair. She looked around the room and the table, and it looked perfect. She quickly walked towards the door, and as she approached the door, her heart fluttered with a mix of excitement and curiosity. This was going to be a very special evening. She took a deep breath, reached for the doorknob, and opened the door slowly.

Standing before her was her man, whose presence seemed to radiate warmth and confidence. He stood tall with an easy grace; his dark hair tousled just enough to give him a rugged charm. His eyes, a deep shade of brown, sparkled with kindness and a hint of mischief as they met hers. A smile spread across his face, genuine and inviting, as he took in her look with appreciation. In that moment, time seemed to pause as they stood there, silently taking each other in. "You look beautiful tonight, Chloe," he said in his deep voice, and pecked her on the cheek as he offered her a single rose and a gift.

Chloe burst into a big smile. He knew that she loved gifts. Her voice exuberated with excitement as she asked him, "What is it?"

"Open it," he said.

Chloe went and sat on the couch nearby. James followed behind her and remained standing. Chloe shook the package excitedly; it was beautifully wrapped. She carefully removed the wrapping and opened the box. As she opened the box slowly, her eyes widened. She gasped and turned to look at James with bewilderment. James loved that look; *it was worth it*, he thought with a smile at the corner of his mouth.

Nestled inside was the most beautiful piece of diamond necklace. It shimmered with stunning brilliance. Its design was elegant and reflected her taste as she held it in her hand. A rush of emotions swept over her—gratitude, joy, and a profound sense of being cherished.

"It's beautiful," she whispered. It was a moment she would never forget, a reminder of love and appreciation that warmed her heart and filled her with excitement for the future moments that they would share. "It's beautiful, James. It is so beautiful," she said, tears welling up in her eyes. She couldn't hold them back anymore.

"The moment I saw it, I thought of you," James said beaming with joy.

"Oh, James! You didn't have to...how can we afford to buy this...I mean, our wedding is in another three weeks, and I thought we had agreed to pool all our resources together."

"Yes, we did," said James, "but I had to make the sacrifice. I really wanted to get this for you, darling."

Chloe tried hard to swallow her tears of joy. She gazed at James with misty eyes, which reflected tremendous love and appreciation. She knew the amount of sacrifice James must have put in to get her this precious gift, and she really cherished it.

"Allow me," said James. He quickly came over to her side and took the necklace from Chloe's hands. Chloe turned her back to him and he put it around her neck. Chloe saw her reflection in a mirror at the farther end of the room, and the necklace dazzled, reflecting the light from the candles. It matched her evening outfit, and she looked stunning.

Chloe turned around and raised her chin and pecked him on his cheek, "You are the best." With a twinkle in her eye and a mischievous smile, she jumped to her feet.

James laughed when he saw Chloe jump from the couch energetically, "I shall take that as a compliment," he said with a boyish grin and ran his hand through his tousled hair. He looked at the set table and said, "So, with that out of the way, hmm... when do we eat? I am famished."

"Dinner is almost ready, darling! But we have to wait for my parents. They should be here any time now," said Chloe as she looked at the clock.

"Dinner with your parents? Again?" exclaimed James.

"Yes, please don't be mad. They insisted, and I couldn't tell them no," she said with a sheepish look.

"It's okay," said James in a resigned tone.

He knew that Chloe's parents were very excited about the upcoming wedding, especially Chloe's mom, Mary. She was very supportive about the whole thing and wanted to help as much as possible with the wedding plans, and at the same time, ensure that she doesn't cause too much interference. She was quite understanding. After all, Chloe was her only daughter and a very precious child.

"Great!" said Chloe, relieved that James was such an understanding person. She briskly walked towards the kitchen to set the food on the table.

Chloe's cooking was always delicious. She picked up the art of cooking delicious, simple meals from her mother James looked appreciatively at all the wonderful dishes that Chloe was setting on the table one by one. "Here, let me help you," he said and walked over to Chloe.

"Oh! That's fine, James. It's nothing at all. Thank you, darling! Why don't you relax for a bit? It's been a long day for you," she said as she hurried back to the kitchen.

"Oh, well! If you say so," said James as he plopped himself on the couch and looked around the room. His gaze fell on the pictured frames on the wall, which drew his attention. He decided to take a closer look and walked up to them. "Strange! I didn't see this photo gallery wall before. Did you put it up recently, Chloe?" he asked.

"Yes, James. I got to finish it yesterday. Take a look."

Chapter 2

In the heart of the living room, nestled among the library of books, a small space was dedicated to harbour the treasure trove of Chloe's memories. The warm glow of candlelight from the dining table flickered over the photo frames.

Pictures of baby Chloe: cuddled in her mother's arms; a toddler Chloe pulling her hair; a school girl Chloe with braided hair, giggling with a toothless smile; a teenage Chloe fishing with her dad; the gorgeous picture of Chloe in her prom dress and Mary beaming with pride, looking at her daughter. Then there was a particular picture that caught his attention.

The picture of Chloe's graduation ceremony. A very important phase in a teenager's life, a big milestone achievement, and a proud moment for the parents. He could see the joy and pride on the faces of Mary and George, Chloe's dad. Years of hard work and support from the family finally paid off on that great, joyous occasion, as the parents cheered the young graduate to the next chapter of her life. There was immense happiness and accomplishment on Mary's face that also reflected a mix of emotions—pride, nostalgia, joy, admiration, and love. It appeared to be Mary's greatest achievement seeing her daughter graduate. Of course, Mary and George went through a lot of challenges in their life while raising Chloe. But in all those storms of life, they ensured that Chloe was never neglected. The difficult days and the sleepless nights in raising baby Chloe to a young beautiful, accomplished college graduate was a great achievement, especially for Mary. These pictures reminded James of how much Mary and George cherished their daughter. All these pictures highlighted an emotional journey that unfolded through the photographs adorning the walls. Each frame captured a fragment of existence, frozen in time yet pulsating with life.

"Pastor asked me to spearhead a production this summer, you know," said Chloe. She looked around and saw that James was engrossed in the picture gallery. She quickly realized that she had already interrupted him, so in a soft voice, she completed her statement, "He wants me to write the script and also direct it."

James slowly turned around, pulled his eyes away from all the moments that were encapsulated in time, and came back to the present, "That's great," he said and looked at Chloe awaiting a response.

She shook her head and said, "I told him I couldn't."

"But why?" he asked, puzzled. It was strange that Chloe rejected the offer, as she was an active and enthusiastic member of the church. *Surely, there must be a good reason*, he thought.

"Well, Netflix has asked me to do a rewrite of the script that I sent them, and they want to see something in two weeks. I think they are seriously considering it," she said. Her eyes twinkled with excitement.

"And that means what exactly?" asked James. He wanted to understand her perspective.

"Well, if they accept the manuscript, I will have to fly out to LA for at least six months." She paused and looked at James, "That's for the preliminary stage production." She wasn't sure how James would take this. She hadn't briefed him about these recent developments. She crossed her fingers and hoped that James would understand.

"Six months!?" James exclaimed, "That's a long time, and my boss will not grant me six months of leave."

"Well," sighed Chloe, she knew she had to be careful with her statements now, "I will have to go without you, darling." She spoke slowly, and quickly walked up to him and looked at him with imploring eyes. She knew this was going to be hard on James, but she was hopeful that he would understand. He had always supported her, encouraged and challenged her to aspire to new heights in her career as a writer. Chloe totally understood what was going on in James' mind. She drew closer to him and held his hand. "James, I—I'm a big girl now. You don't have to be so overprotective anymore. I can manage on my own. Please don't worry, darling. Six months will just fly away in no time. It is not a year. This is for the greater good. I can't turn back on this opportunity, James, and besides, this...this is the reason I was born. I am positive about this."

James knew with the tone of her voice that this meant a lot to her, and she had worked very hard for this, but six months felt really long for him at the moment. "I know how passionate you are about this story, Chloe," he said with gentleness in his voice.

"It is not just any story, James." She paused, "It was inspired by God. I want people to see and understand the level of sacrifice that Jesus made for us. He died so we might have life."

"I am a pastor's son, Chloe. I am aware of what we believe." James was convinced at an early stage in his young adult life, that he would get married to a woman who had a strong belief in Christ Jesus and Christian values. He prayed that the Lord would direct his path and he would meet his life partner, the one chosen by God for him. He was very happy that the Lord led him to meet Chloe, who shared the same belief and dedication to Christ and His teachings. She also had a tremendous zeal and burden to spread the gospel to the unreached at every opportunity that came her way, in her own creative way.

"Then, understand that if God wants me to go, I have to," said Chloe with determination in her voice.

"Well, that doesn't mean I have to like it," said James, and he walked towards the window.

Chloe understood that it was very difficult for James, especially after they had planned for their future in a certain way and this was happening right after the wedding. It was hard on James to be separated from Chloe for so long and it was equally hard on her too. She will miss him, miss his companionship. *Perhaps, if there was an opportunity, I could fly and spend the weekend with him or vice versa,* she thought. There can always be a workaround. God would make the way for her, even though it looked impossible. She knew that it was God who had led her thus far. He was bound to meet all her needs, for her priority was to ensure that the message of hope and salvation would reach out to as many people as possible, and Netflix was a big platform, a big opportunity.

Chloe walked closer to James and wrapped her hands around him, resting her cheek on his chest, "I love you, James. You know that, and nothing will change that," she said with reassurance.

"Yeah, I know, Chloe," whispered James. Chloe lifted her head and smiled at him, and he smiled back, lowered his head, and kissed her lips softly.

Just then, the door opened. Mary and George walked in. Caught unaware of the sudden entry, Chloe hurriedly released herself from James and turned around to see who entered. "Oh, hi, mother," she exclaimed.

"Are we interrupting anything?" said Mary with a glint of mischief in her eyes and smiles. "I can't get used to the fact that you're a grown woman now, Chloe, and I'm supposed to knock at your door before entering." Mary chuckled, amused by Chloe's frantic efforts to look normal.

"How are you, Mary?" asked James, as he greeted his mother-in-law with a peck on her cheek.

Mary looked at James with great admiration and pride, "I am very well, thank you, James." Mary always had a soft corner for James, and she had hoped in her heart that Chloe and James would one day be together and live a happily-ever-after life. James, being the son of their church pastor, was actively involved in various outreach programs organized by the church, and Mary could see the passion he had for Christ. He was a man with strong Christian beliefs and great integrity—*the perfect match for Chloe,* she thought.

"How's my girl?" George said in his deep voice and walked up to his daughter. George was equally thrilled that James and Chloe made a wonderful pair. He looked lovingly at his daughter, realizing that she had grown up to be a beautiful, elegant woman.

"I am cool, dad," said Chloe. She smiled and held his strong hand, and planted a kiss on his forehead.

George looked at James and greeted him as well, "And my son-in-law?"

"Err, I am cool too!" said James sheepishly as he ran his hand through his hair, "Hmm, can we eat now?" He said, looking at the table that was set with all the delicious food.

George burst into laughter and said, "Of course. You look famished. Come on now, let's eat."

So, George and Mary, James and Chloe sat together around the table laughing, and there was an air of celebration, joy, and excitement in the room.

Chapter 3

"It was a great dinner," said Mary as she slipped into the warm bedcovers. They had returned quite late from the dinner. Time flew by and they didn't realize how late it was. They had so much to talk about, and yes, above all, Mary was quite pleased with Chloe's culinary talent.

"Yes, I agree. Had a lovely time with them. My sweet child is going to a bride soon," said George. "How fast she grew up. Can't imagine...it only seemed like yesterday when I held her in my arms, a small bundle of joy. Now the time is coming soon when I have to walk her down the aisle to give my baby to her husband." George was a little nostalgic.

Both Mary and George lay in their bed, taking their moment to allow the fact to sink in—that their darling daughter is now a grown-up, mature, independent lady who was going to be a wife soon. While Mary thought about the time she had with Chloe—the time she helped her choose her prom dress and got her ready for her very first prom; George lay on his side of the bed and thought about the time he had with his daughter—when he taught her how to fix the car tire. It was a lot of fun and memorable moments.

"Good night, darling," said George as he turned around to turn off the lights.

"Good night, George," said Mary, and she turned to her side to sleep.

It had been more than an hour, but sleep seemed to evade Mary. She tossed and turned but couldn't sleep. She stared at the window in her bedroom. The soft breeze made the curtains move lightly and the moonlight to fall into the room. She thought it must be due to all the excitement that she couldn't sleep. After much time, she dozed off.

"Mother, I love you mother!" Mary could hear Chloe's voice from a distance.

"Yes, Chloe, where are you?" It appeared as if Mary could hear Chloe's voice, but it sounded far off. Mary got off her bed, opened her door and entered the living room. She turned on the lights but no one was there. Then she heard Chloe's voice again; this time, it sounded nearer to her.

Chloe's voice said, "At first, it was hard for me to understand, but as time passed, I began to see the reasoning behind your choice. Your choice, mother!" There was a pause, and again the voice said, "Still, you don't just destroy the life of someone you love, right?"

Mary didn't understand. She looked around and said, "Chloe, what are you talking about?"

Chloe continued to say, "I questioned your love for a long time. I know you were young, confused, full of fear, but is there really a good reason to do what you did? I don't think so. I am told to forgive, but how do I do that exactly?"

"Forgive? Chloe, what are you talking about?" Mary said and frantically looked around to catch a glimpse of Chloe but in vain. She ran to the door to open and see if Chloe was there but didn't find anyone. She shut the door and scanned the room.

She was bewildered, frightened, unable to comprehend what she heard. Many thoughts rushed into her mind. She felt numb.

She couldn't utter a word. It seemed as if she was paralyzed by the shock and was speechless. She only shook her head in disbelief. Finally, she managed to utter in a small breathless voice, "No, no, Chloe. Noooo!" She screamed and opened her eyes into pitch darkness. Mary was out of breath. She gasped and sprung up.

George got jostled, and he woke up with a jolt. "What happened? Mary, what happened?" he asked and turned to the side to turn on the light.

Mary looked a bit pale. Her lips trembled. She muttered, "Nightmare, I just had a nightmare." She turned to her side and reached out for a glass of water. Her hand shook as she held her glass of water and gulped it down hastily. The water spilled on her and on her bedspread. Mary took a deep breath to try and settle her rattled nerves. "It's okay, George. It was only a nightmare. I am alright now. Please go back to sleep. I am sorry."

"Oh, poor darling," said George. "You will be okay." He kissed Mary on her forehead and turned around to get back to sleep. He wasn't sure what the nightmare was, but he thought it would be better to talk about it in the morning.

Mary lay on her side but couldn't sleep. Sleep just evaded her. She was troubled to her very soul; she couldn't understand why. As she mulled over her dream, beads of perspiration broke over her forehead. She replayed what she heard in her mind. *This couldn't be,* she thought. *What a strange dream! It felt quite sinister.* She tried to brush it off, but those words echoed in her head louder and louder, "It was your choice, right? Your choice! Your choice." Mary shook her head in an attempt to stop the voice in her ears, but it was pointless. She started to pray in her mind with the hope that it would stop. "Our Father, Which art in heaven. Hallowed be Thy Name. Thy Kingdome come, Thy will be done on Earth as it is in Heaven. Give us this day our daily bread, and forgive us our sins as we forgive those who sin against us…"

Suddenly, she was reminded of what she heard in her dream—"I am told to forgive, but how do I do that exactly?" Chloe's voice rang in her head.

Mary shook her head again to get the voice off her mind and resumed to utter the prayer, this time softly…"Lead us not into temptation. But deliver us from evil, for Thine is the Kingdom and the power and glory, forever and ever. Amen."

She continued to repeat the prayer until she fell asleep.

Chapter 4

It had been a week since Mary spoke to Chloe.

It was early evening; Mary was preparing some tea when she heard the doorbell ring. She looked on her CCTV and saw Chloe at the door. She rushed to open the door quickly and welcomed Chloe in. Chloe looked very excited, as if she had some great information to share with her mother.

"Hi, Mom! I was afraid I might miss meeting you today. Sorry I couldn't call and let you know. I was in a hurry." Chloe spoke rapidly as she hugged her mother.

Mary calmed her down, "Chloe, you are quite excited today. It looks like you have something exciting going on. Here, let me take your coat," she said and hung the coat behind the entry door. "Why don't you settle down on the couch while I get you some tea."

Mary went to get a cup of tea for Chloe. Chloe settled down on the couch and quickly grabbed her tote bag, rummaged through it, and started to take out a lot of papers. Mary was a bit quizzical, unsure of what Chloe wanted to tell her.

"Mother, I wanted to talk to you about the topic I had been researching for my Netflix assignment. I wanted to hear your perspectives and also see if I can get some good information for this assignment."

"Sure, darling," said Mary. She always loved it when her daughter wanted to get her involved in certain matters of great importance. "Let's see what we can come up with." Mary was excited.

Chloe pulled out a bunch of papers, scrambled through them, and picked out one paper. She wore her glasses and read through for a while silently, and handed it over to Mary. Mary read through the paper that was handed to her, and after some time, she put it down on the coffee table. She got up from the couch and walked slowly towards the kitchen counter to put the empty cups in the kitchen sink.

"Well? What do you think, Mom?" asked Chloe in a surprised tone. Her mother's silence felt strange to her.

Mary took a deep breath, paused for a moment and said, "I know there is a strong possibility that abortion is wrong no matter which angle you look at it, but it is still the choice of the parents," said Mary, carefully choosing her words.

"I don't disagree with you. It's just that all angles have to be explored objectively to make people understand why it is wrong. It is not enough to just say, 'don't do this,' without stating why; and I believe that it is 'why' that separates good parenting from bad parenting," said Chloe in an emphatic tone.

"This is not a topic I am comfortable talking about. Can't we discuss something else?" Mary sounded quite unsettled, and Chloe noticed that.

"There are people out there who need to understand what they are considering when they think about abortion," Chloe said.

"I see," said Mary seeing that she has no other way out but to sit through this discussion, even though it was an uncomfortable topic.

"I have conducted my own research. Are you interested enough to listen to what I have discovered?"

Mary could hear the excitement in Chloe's voice. "I guess I am. I have nothing else to do right now."

"Great! This is the testimony of a young Christian at the Bethel Baptist Church," Chloe pulled out a file and started to read from it.

"She was sharing at a convention they had three years ago and I recorded it, for reference. She said I could use it to help spread the word. Here, let me read it out for you." Chloe adjusted her glasses and her voice, *"I had never heard of such a thing. Kill the life within me? This was not some blob of tissue I could have had dissected and discarded at will, but a separate living being. We had distinct blood types. I heard his heartbeat. He jumped when he had hiccups; he was agitated and kicked when I ate garlic. Abortion was no option. I can't say it has been easy these past years; God intended that there be two parents. But every time I look into my girl's big brown eyes, or hear her "Mommy, I love you," I know I was right. Best thing that has ever happened to me. So, what if I got a late start on my education? So what if I don't have time to socialize, with the many demands upon my time? Single parents have twice the responsibility and half the help. I know I have hugs and kisses that no money can buy. No, what's convenient is not always best, or right. Easy street is a dead end. What if Jesus Christ had only been thinking of himself, and his 'right,' when it came time to go to the cross? Calvary was not convenient, but interrupted His career—big time. God is forgiving, and we all make mistakes. But there are choices we will have to live with for the rest of our lives. The choice I live with has a name, a smile, a birthday, and a future. All abortion had to offer was a dead baby. What kind of 'choice' is that?"*

After reading it out, Chloe quietly placed the file down. There was a silence in the room. It appeared as if both mother and daughter were taking their moment to gather their thoughts and the weight of the story lingered in the air; it felt heavy.

Chloe cleared her throat and said slowly, "She was sixteen at the time and the daughter of a Bishop, so you can imagine what she went through."

"What happened to her?" Mary asked. She was curious.

"She moved to Florida last year, with her beautiful baby girl. She named her Chiemeka, an African name which means 'God has performed a great Deed.'"

Mary seemed to be lost in deep thought, "Did her father kick her out?" she asked.

"Not directly, but apparently, he couldn't tolerate her 'mistake.'"

"What about the baby's father?" Suddenly, Mary felt she had so many questions, and it was difficult to hide her curiosity about this girl, who took a daring step to protect her baby and boldly raised her.

"Gone, as usual, but the Lord is really working it out for her. She now has a job and will be registering for evening classes soon. Who knows what her child will become in the future," said Chloe in a matter-of-fact tone.

"Well, that doesn't change the fact that abortion is a personal choice," Mary sounded defiant.

"Who gave us the right to choose if a baby lives or dies? Only God is entitled to determine the end of one's life. The deliberate destruction of human life without cause is sin, punishable by death." Chloe sounded a bit angry.

"Now that is the question that we need to answer," said Mary immediately, "At what stage is a baby a baby, or more so a living being?"

Chloe looked at Mary with disbelief and bewilderment. She couldn't understand why her mother was unable to recognize the obvious.

"Scripture does not refer to the unborn as blobs of tissue, but as children. In Luke 1:36, we read that Elizabeth had "conceived a son." In Mathew 1:18, 23, Mary is said to be "with child." When Rebecca conceived twins, it says, "the children struggled together within her." The unborn child is able to sense such feelings as "joy." In Luke 1:44-45, Elizabeth's babe leaped in her womb for joy. The unborn babe, independent of the mother, made movements, so "it" cannot be reduced to merely a "part of the woman's body"--a necessary step in reducing the issue to that of a "woman's right." When Rebecca conceived, "the children struggled together within her." They struggled not she. This reinforces the fact that the unborn child is a separate being apart from the mother. Even some basic personal characteristics of individuals are determined before birth. Of Jacob, whose name means supplanter, we read: 'he' (implying personhood) took his brother (also implying personhood, based on their biological relationship), by the heel in the womb. God has a plan for each life, established at conception. Jeremiah 1:5 'while you were being formed in the belly of the womb,' God told the prophet Jeremiah. 'I knew you and ordained (intended for) you to be a prophet to the nations.' Another quote, 'The Lord hath called me from the womb, from the bowels of my mother hath he made mention of my name, to be his servant, to bring Jacob again unto him.' In Galatians 1:15, Paul said he was 'called from my mother's womb.' The psalmist wrote of being 'formed in secret,' in his mother's womb, referring to himself in such a state, 'yet imperfect (incomplete),' as "I"—that is, a person."

Chloe paused and took a breath. She was astonished at the way in which she delivered the whole message. It was as if the words had just come out of her mouth without any effort, and it had gone out like a double-edged sword that put to rest every thought and idea that was not in accordance with the Word of God. There was silence in the room.

"Wow, you have really done your research. You present some strong and interesting points, but I'm sure that the State doesn't care much about biblical truths," said Mary thoughtfully.

"Someone has to."

"Yes, but you can't change the world," said Mary.

"Maybe not, but I serve someone who can," said Chloe, her voice resounding the confidence she had in her faith.

"You really buy into all this Jesus stuff?" Mary asked.

Chloe was amazed to hear such a statement from her mother. She thought that her mother shared the same faith, but somewhere her words sounded as if she was cynical, only because she wanted to defend her idealogies.

"Yes, Mom, I do, and I think you should too," said Chloe, intently looking at her mother.

"I hear that the Lord is a patient man. When the right time comes, it will happen," Mary said as she brushed off Chloe's intense looks.

"Time does not belong to us, Mom."

"Well, that's what you keep saying, but it's obvious we have some control over time. You wouldn't be here right now if we didn't," said Mary.

Chloe didn't know what else to say. It appeared as if the conversation was leading nowhere. She felt a little distant and couldn't connect with her mother.

"Your philosophies are interesting, but they are not biblical," said Chloe as she gathered all her paperwork that was spread on the coffee table and put them into her bag.

"Well, not everything is written in that Bible of yours."

"Who said we had to agree on everything, right?" Chloe said in an attempt to end the conversation on a nicer tone and remove that air of discomfort in the room.

"Right. I have to start dinner early, Chloe. We are leaving for Miami early tomorrow morning. It would be nice if you could stay back for dinner as well."

"Thank you, Mom, but I have a busy day tomorrow. It was nice that I could spend the evening with you and thank you for sharing your thoughts and opinions and taking the time to listen to what I had to say. Love you, Mom." Chloe walked up to the door.

"Sure, baby, have a good night. Talk to you soon," said Mary as she hugged Chloe. Mary walked her to the door and waved goodbye.

Mary went back to her kitchen counter and started to fix dinner for George and herself. George had mentioned in the morning that he could be home a bit early since they had to leave for Miami early next morning. All the packing required for the trip was already done. It was just a matter of looking around to fix any last-minute things and get going.

As Mary started to prepare her dinner, her mind kept wandering back to the discussions she had with Chloe in the evening. She couldn't stop playing in her mind the story of the young girl who made the choice of keeping her child and faced the challenges of being a single parent early in life, very boldly and courageously. And how she was really happy with her decision and with no regrets.

Mary reminisced about her own experience. She could see the day she held the pregnancy test in her hand with the positive result. She knew her life would never be the same. Thoughts flooded her mind; she had her own story to tell. *"When I found out I was pregnant, it was not a 'convenient' time. I was still in school; my mother was unemployed; we had no insurance, and we had just been evicted. We didn't even have the money to move. Too proud to turn to welfare, we simply did without. No running water. No heat. Canned goods froze in the cupboard. Water in the sink (from snow I had melted) became solid overnight. I was a thousand miles from any other family and didn't have a friend in town. Naïve was I to think I had no choice."* Mary let out a deep sigh. *The past is past, nothing can change it now. Now it is all about moving on in life, and focus on Chloe's upcoming wedding. Besides, it happened a long time back.* She shook herself up, determined to focus on getting the dinner fixed and arrest her wandering mind that seemed to delve into the things of the past.

Chapter 5

Chloe was up and early; it was a bright and sunny, beautiful day. She was busy putting things together to leave. She checked her baggage and then double-checked again to ensure she didn't forget anything.

Her very being radiated the excitement and thrill. This was her dream project—a great opportunity that God had placed in her lap—to be able to tell the story, to reach a wider audience on the most important issue that is plaguing today's society. She hoped and prayed that this would have a bigger and greater impact on the lives of the people who watch it. That they will understand the seriousness and have the boldness to make wise choices.

"I thought you would be ready," the voice of James broke through her thoughts.

"Almost. I want to make sure I don't leave anything," said Chloe as she looked around her bedroom.

"So, you're really going, huh?" asked James, knowing that nothing can change now.

"I have to, James. Please, let's not have an argument again about this."

"Okay, okay. It's just that..." he trailed off. James didn't complete his sentence, and Chloe knew what was going on in his mind.

It was difficult for him to stay away from her, especially so soon after marriage. They had planned many things, but somehow, this Netflix project wasn't featured in the blueprint of their plans.

Chloe stopped doing what she was doing for a second. She walked up to James and kissed him on his cheek. "I will miss you too, my dear husband," said Chloe with a big smile on her face which cheered James.

"Alright then, hurry up before you miss your flight." James carried her baggage to the door. Chloe was busy again. She stacked the manuscripts into a briefcase and looked through some files for relevant paperwork.

"How long before this movie of yours comes out?" asked James.

"Maybe two- or three-years, darling."

"Wow! That long?" James was surprised.

"Yes, it's a process. There's still some rewriting to do before the script is production-ready."

"Well, at least we'll be able to buy that house you always dreamed of."

"Oh yeah, and make a valuable contribution to your new church building," said Chloe suddenly with a lost look on her face, as if she is already in the future.

"Yeah, and get a whole new set of golf clubs," said James with a chuckle.

That statement brought Chloe back to her present, "Oh! Don't push it, James" she said with a playful scowl on her face. James couldn't help but burst with a hearty boy's laugh when he saw that silly expression on her face.

"Alright, alright. Okay, let's get these bags out. They seem quite heavy," he said as he dragged the heavy bags through the exit. Chloe looked around one last time to make sure that she didn't forget anything. Before she could exit the door, she said one last prayer, "Okay, Lord. This is it. You know I can't do this alone, so please don't forget me in this time of my need." She sighed and closed the door behind her.

They had a silent drive to the airport. James was lost in his thoughts. As he glanced at Chloe, his heart was swollen with gratitude. He had spent his whole life searching for that perfect relationship, that one true love that God had reserved just for him. He couldn't see his life without her. It would be a miserable reality if someone thought God had made a mistake when Chloe was conceived. Yes, God punishes us for our sins, but even the consequences of our actions work for the greater good in the long run. Regardless, Chloe was the best thing that had ever happened to him, and he would cherish every single moment he had with her.

"Are you okay?" Chloe's question pulled James back into the present moment.

"I'm gonna miss you, babe," James gave an encouraging but difficult smile.

Chapter 6

It was early evening. Chloe's apartment bustled with a lot of activity and excitement. Mary, George, and James were all there in her apartment. They were here to celebrate the success of Chloe's Netflix project. It was hard to believe that time flew so quickly.

Chloe had worked with great resilience and passion towards the project. She was grateful to James who stood steadfast and supported her all the way through, even though it was difficult for them to stay apart for all those months. Chloe had worked late nights and long hours, but eventually, it all paid off. Now here they were, all together, celebrating Chloe's achievement, the accomplishment of her dream project.

George reached out for his wine glass. "I would like to make a toast." Everyone reached for their glasses. "To the greatest Christian screenwriter of the 21st century."

"Here, here!" Everyone raised their glasses to toast.

"I will drink to that," said James.

"I am a changed man because of you, Chloe," George said. He looked adoringly at his daughter and was proud of her success.

"Amen!" Mary shouted. She sounded exhilarated.

"God deserves the glory," said Chloe as she beamed at her dad.

"I told you when the time was right," said Mary.

George quickly completed her sentence, "Yes, nothing happens before its time."

"Have you seen yesterday's newspaper, Chloe?" George asked as he looked around to get ahold of one.

"No, I did not."

"Well, here...take a look," said James as he eagerly handed over one to Chloe. Chloe read the headlines, and slowly, tears started to build in her eyes. She was overwhelmed by the response and support she received from the audience. The reviews from various media sources were astounding.

"Hollywood is flabbergasted," said George, "at the level of support your movie received. The churches across the world have been seeing a steady increase in attendance. Everyone knows your name now, Chloe."

"I can't believe this. I never expected this kind of, this kind of...blessing."

"The Lord has favoured you, my love," said James as he looked at his wife with love and beamed with pride at her success.

"Well, most importantly, you have opened our eyes to the truth of the gospel. I knew it theoretically, but experiencing it is a completely different thing," said Mary. Her eyes had an intense look. It appeared as if she was lost in thought, gone to some past, and there appeared to be a sparkle of life in her eyes now. "Your story has changed lives, Chloe. That's why we are here." She sounded pensive.

"My sentiments exactly," said George.

As the family continued to absorb and celebrate the success of the movie, there was a knock at the door. *Who could it be at this time?* James got up quickly to answer the door. He came back with a very large bag filled with letters, "This is from the post office...today's mail." he said. "It just came in, and it would seem that it's all for you, Chloe."

"All of this?" exclaimed Chloe. She had never seen so much mail in all her life. James placed the bag in front of her. Chloe took a step back and covered her mouth with her hands, overwhelmed. She just had to find a spot to sit. "Just for today," said James. He smiled as he looked at her.

"Well, I suggest you get a head start, honey. Come tomorrow, a haulage truck may have to bring your mail," said George as he winked at Chloe and laughed as he flung his hands into the thin air. They lifted their glasses one more time and shared a good laugh.

"To the perfect life," Mary said.

"I'll drink to that," said James.

"Hear, hear," said George, and they all raised a toast.

The atmosphere was filled with jubilation, happiness, and excitement. As the evening unfolded amidst the celebration, Chloe's achievement continued to resonate. What seemed to be an impossible task, God made it possible for her to finish it with great excellence and passion. Her willingness to obey her calling, even though it seemed difficult, eventually paid off. She was able to spread the good news to a larger audience.

Chapter 7

It was the next day, after the celebration of the tremendous success of Chloe's movie. Mary was getting ready to go to Chloe's place to help her with the mail. She was in good spirits, although they had a late night. Mary couldn't wait to get to the pile of mail and read all the wonderful things that people had to say about her daughter's movie. She felt so thankful to God, and it meant so much for her. She quickly brushed her hair, put on her favourite lipstick, and looked at herself just one more time in the mirror before she headed out to the door. George went to work that day, so he couldn't come by to help Mary and Chloe with all that mail. But he did offer to pick up Mary once they were done.

Mary reached Chloe's place, rang the doorbell, and waited. But there was no answer. *That's strange,* she thought. She had informed Chloe the previous night that she would drop by to help her with all the mail around early afternoon. She rang the bell one more time. Still no response. She turned the doorknob, and to her surprise, the door opened. She stumbled into the living room, and her eyes fell on Chloe.

What she saw visibly shook her. Chloe was seated on the couch, crying uncontrollably. Some letters were in her hands, but a huge chunk was still in the PO bag, untouched. Mary was extremely concerned, unable to understand what was going on.

Were people so nasty to write such mails that got my baby crying, she thought. She ran towards Chloe with her hands outstretched in an attempt to comfort her, "Oh, baby! What happened?"

"Don't you baby me!" Chloe snapped, scaring Mary a bit.

Mary was confused. "Wha...what has gotten into you? What's wrong?" she asked, unable to comprehend what was going on.

"Why! Why have you allowed me to live a lie?" yelled Chloe.

Mary looked stunned. She didn't know how to respond. She blinked hard at Chloe, "What are you talking about, my child?"

"I am not your child," said Chloe in a jeering way.

"What? How can you say that?" gasped Mary.

"You are not my mother. These letters," Chloe throws the letters at Mary, "These letters are not real. This house... this life... my life. It's all an illusion," Chloe screamed.

The flurry of words that came out of Chloe frightened Mary. She had never seen Chloe like this. So distraught. Mary was unable to grasp what was troubling Chloe. "Chloe, you are not making sense," said Mary, trying to regain her composure as she tried to absorb all that Chloe threw at her.

"You made this all up, mother. You created this perfect world in your mind. This perfect life doesn't exist because I am dead. I am dead, mother! And you killed me!" shouted Chloe, and burst into uncontrollable sobs of anger.

Mary went pale. A corner of her mouth started to quiver. She didn't know what this was all about. "Okay, okay. You know what, you are freaking me out right about now. Maybe if you calmed down," said Mary. Her mouth went dry. Nothing made sense. She wondered if Chloe lost her mind, unable to handle the spotlight of her success.

"This perfect life doesn't exist because I am dead, mother," she said with bitterness ringing in her voice. "I am dead and you killed me, mother!, Chloe said with a cold look directed towards Mary. "Wake up, mother! You took my life away before it even began. Wake up!" Chloe was shouting.

"Will you stop shouting at me," Mary screamed as she closed her ears with her hands. What she heard from Chloe sounded so absurd, so unreal. Mary was confused and bewildered. It felt like she lost touch with reality.

"Wake up!" shouted Chloe. Mary tried to hold Chloe, but she wrestled with her. She could hear the words "Wake up!" like a chant, and her world seemed to reel around her. Everything seemed to spin, and Mary felt as if she was getting sucked into a sinkhole. She was engulfed in dizziness. She started to black out. She reached out to Chloe in desperation, but all she heard was Chloe's voice, "You killed me! Wake up! This is all a lie." It resonated with cruelty in her ears, and everything dimmed out.

Chapter 8

Mary didn't know for how long she was unconscious. She faintly heard Chloe's voice again, "Wake up." It felt as if she spoke to her from a distance.

"Wake up, Mary." This time it was a man's voice. Again, the voice rang, "Mary, wake up!"

Mary slowly opened her eyes, coming out of her blackness, but she felt the room spin. She closed her eyes and again opened them slowly. Her vision slowly started to clear, and for a moment, she couldn't remember where she was or why. She looked around and tried to understand her surroundings. She saw a man standing close to her. He wore a dark tweed slacks and a white lab coat, with a notepad in his hands. He seemed to be making brisk notes. He looked like a doctor to her.

Mary realized that she was seated in a wheelchair. She had no clue why she was in a wheelchair and what happened that got her to this place. She noticed the doctor watch her closely while she wrestled with the reality of where she was.

"Where am I?" Mary asked with a shake in her voice.

"You don't remember where you are?" asked the man in the white coat. Mary tried to get up, but she couldn't, and she fell out of the wheelchair. The doctor quickly called out to the nurse, and they helped her back into the wheelchair.

"My legs, my legs," said Mary in an alarmed tone and her voice quivered, "I can't feel my legs." She looked around with panic on her face.

"I know, I know, Mary," the doctor said, "Just try to relax, Mary, it will all come back to you," he said in a reassuring tone.

"Chloe! Where is my daughter Chloe?" she panicked.

The doctor seemed to brush away her question. "Try to relax, Mary," the doctor said, and he scribbled away in his notepad.

Infuriated, Mary yelled, looking at him, "Stop telling me to relax and just answer the question. Who are you by the way?"

"I am, err, your doctor," he replied patiently, and there was calmness in his voice.

Mary looked around to see if she could see anyone familiar. She hoped to catch a glimpse of Chloe's face. But no one at all. She looked down at her legs and tried to lift herself from the wheelchair, and she felt that it needed an unusual amount of strength—both mental and physical—but she couldn't lift herself. With a confused look, she asked, "What's wrong with my legs?" She tried to maintain a steady voice but couldn't.

"You are temporarily paralyzed, Mary," the doctor said.

Her voice trembled, "What! How?" with disbelief on her face.

"Mary, I can't go over this with you every single day. If you will just sit back and relax, you will remember," he said in a matter-of-fact tone and returned to his notes.

Mary took his queue and attempted to relax. She rubbed her forehead, and she felt her stomach churn and turn into a lump. She felt faint. "Why can't I remember?" she asked feebly.

"The accident...you are suffering deep mental trauma, temporary paralysis, amnesia, and disassociation," the doctor replied.

"Amnesia? Accident?" Mary echoed.

"Yes, but you've improved much over the past few days."

"I don't have amnesia. How could I? Just recently I had an argument with my daughter. She was yelling at me. Can you believe that? I am her mother, and she was yelling at me. I remember that pretty well," said Mary confidently.

"Mary, you have no daughter," the doctor said slowly.

As soon as she heard this, she was filled with horror, and a chill hit her spine. She felt the flesh at the back of her neck crawl. She tried to process what she heard; the harsh words that rang in her ear. All of a sudden, she was engulfed in rage and frustration, "What?" she yelled, "Maybe you are the one who needs a doctor. What kind of a doctor are you anyway?

"I am a psychiatrist," he replied.

Mary wanted to scream but was unable to. This was unthinkable. She was terrified with every piece of information that was given to her. "A shrink?! Why do I need a shrink?" There was a tone of dismay in her voice.

"You have been through a lot, Mary. Maybe I should cancel today's session and we come back tomorrow," the doctor said.

"But why do I need a shrink?" Mary asked with a tone of persistence.

The doctor paused before he replied. He took a moment and slowly responded, "You have been suffering from deep psychological trauma, clinical depression, short-term amnesia, and disassociation. Your brain is playing tricks on you, making you illusional at best, and I think you have some neuropsychiatric illness. Plus, you fell down a twenty-step stairway three days ago after you and your husband had a fight," he paused for Mary to absorb each piece of information, especially with the medical terms.

Mary's mouth dropped open. She looked numb and motionless, with disbelief and shock on her face.

She repeated again to comprehend what she heard; her eyes seemed to be looking at something distant. "Me and my husband had a fight? Oh! Maybe that's why Chloe was so mad. We weren't getting along at all," she said and had a dazed look.

She heard her doctor sigh loudly, and she shifted her attention to him and looked straight in his eye. "Mary, there is no Chloe. Never has been, maybe never will be. Chloe DOESN'T exist," he said with great intensity and firmness in his voice, as if this was the umpteenth time he had to repeat.

"Will you stop saying that please? We are talking about my daughter," said Mary. She obviously sounded horrified. She felt faint and just hoped that this was another nightmare.

The doctor walked closer to her. He lowered himself to look into her eyes. Mary's eyes darted as she tried to focus and get an answer for all the trauma she was going through. The doctor looked as if he didn't want to put Mary through this again. But he had no option, and he wished he didn't have to say the next few words. With a deliberate tone, he says, "Chloe was never born, Mary. You, you had an abortion."

Mary gasped! Her heart skipped a beat. Her head spun, and the helpless feeling of being sucked into a sinkhole kicked in again. She gasped for breath as she heard the brutal statement cut through her soul. "What!" she said with a bewildered look on her face.

"That's why you need a shrink," said the doctor with compassion and tenderness in his voice. As much as it was hard for him to disclose this to Mary, he knew it was equally cruel on her. He could see the pain and agony that swept through her face. She looked devastated, and yes, she was devastated, but *how many times would she have to go through this,* he thought.

"What are you saying?" Mary whimpered; her throat felt dry. She seemed to be drained of all energy, even the little that she had. The doctor handed her a glass of water. She refused, but then she took it. Her hands trembled, and she took a sip. She handed the glass back to him.

"I really don't want to repeat what I just said, Mary," he said. There was a deafening silence in the room.

"I had an abortion?" Mary shook her head in disbelief. "How could I? Chloe helped me to see that abortion was wrong; that in God's eyes, it was a terrible sin. It was murder. Now you're saying I murdered my child?" she cried and buried her face in her hands.

"We are far beyond the stage of denial, Mary. I think it's time you started to accept responsibility for your actions so we can apply the proper procedures necessary to help you."

"If—if what you say is true, if I...did that to my child, you cannot help me, doctor." The pangs of pain crushed her heart. Her child—her Chloe—never existed?

"What do you suggest I do then?" he asked with remorse. He could see the pain in her eyes. Her anguish consumed her whole being. He knew she went through hell, every time. He felt very sorry for her. *God! How many times will she go through this?* He thought in his mind.

"Just go, please," said Mary in a feeble voice.

"We will pick up from here tomorrow, Mary. Please take your medications before you go to bed," he said as he picked up his things, and closed his office door softly.

Chapter 9

Mary, left alone in the doctor's office, tried to absorb all the conversation she had with the doctor. Unable to believe what transpired between them. *Should she trust this man? Is it really true?* She looked around, but there was no George, no Chloe, no James. No one was there.

"Oh, God! What did I just hear? Is it true? Did I kill my child—Chloe?" said Mary aloud with a loud sigh of anguish in her voice and buried her face in the palm of her hands. She shook her head vigorously, unable to accept. If only someone could tell her that this was not true, and all this was just a nightmare and she will get back to be with her beloved daughter, Chloe. Tears streamed down her face as she lifted her head and again looked around the room helplessly. She cried aloud, "Oh, God! Please help me!" She wept uncontrollably.

Suddenly, she heard the door behind her open. Mary hoped to see Chloe's face. Perhaps God did hear her, and this was just a nightmare. *All this would be over, if only I could see Chloe,* she thought as she looked expectantly towards the door. The door opened, and a figure stood before her.

It was not Chloe but a man who stood before her. He loomed tall above her wheelchair. She felt aghast. It wasn't Chloe, her child. She had no clue who this person was.

"Hi, Mary," he said with warmth in his voice.

Mary looked at him in an attempt to identify who he was, but couldn't recognize him, nor was she interested to converse with him at this time. She was emotionally and physically exhausted and felt drained. "I am not taking any more visitors today. Thanks for dropping by," she said and lowered her eyes as she tried to hide the tears from him.

"My name is Alex Brown," he said. "Pastor Alex Brown. I am father to James Brown and a friend of your husband George," he said calmly. Mary quickly raised her eyes when she heard the name James—*my daughter Chloe's husband,* she thought with hope in her eyes. After all, maybe whatever she heard from the doctor was untrue. Here he stood before her—the father of her daughter's husband. Mary turned to look at this man with a glimmer of hope that he might throw some light.

"You are Jame's father?" asked Mary with a hopeful voice.

"Yes, ma'am," said Alex.

"James is the husband of my daughter, Chloe," said Mary to affirm.

"Err, yes. So I've heard," said Alex hesitatingly. There was a long silence in the room. Mary tried to formulate her next question in her mind, and Alex waited patiently for her to ask.

"You are a pastor, a man of truth. You wouldn't lie to me, would you?" Mary asked frantically.

"No, ma'am."

"Please call me Mary," she said with irritation in her voice. *Why is Alex not calling me by my first name, like he always did?* she thought.

"Okay, Mary, I don't lie."

"Is what they say about my daughter true? Chloe is her name, you know. Is it true?" Mary looked at him. She scanned his face and hoped that she would hear what she wanted to hear.

There was an awkward silence in the room. Alex didn't respond to her immediately. It appeared as if he wished he didn't have to say this, but sometimes it is the pastors who have to disclose the harsh truth.

"Yes, I am afraid it is," he said. He knew that would tear her apart.

Mary broke down. She cried inconsolably with bitter tears. "I killed my daughter! But why?" She sounded exasperated.

"You were young, broke, confused, lost maybe. If I was in your position, I probably would have done the same thing," he said earnestly.

"You would?" Mary asked with disbelief.

"Yes, but that still doesn't make it right," he said soberly.

"My daughter, Chloe, was the key to my salvation—my perfect gift. She was the key that would have set free thousands of lost souls," Mary stopped, unable to continue. Her voice choked. "I took that away because I was just thinking about myself."

"She still is the key," Alex said immediately. "It is not too late for you to accept Jesus into your heart, Mary. You know Chloe's story better than anyone else. You need to tell it." His voice expressed an urgency.

But Mary couldn't understand what Alex said. She was still in the past. "It would have been rough the first few years, but then everything would have been perfect." She sounded lost.

"Listen to me, Mary," Alex held shoulders and tried to get her back to her present, "Chloe is resting in the bosom of Jesus

Christ, even as we speak. You don't have to be eternally separated from your daughter, or from your Creator."

"But I don't know what to do." Mary said thoughtfully. It seemed to have dawned on her that she went through this cycle of amnesia and came back to face reality. And every such episode was so traumatic to her. The magnitude of the impact, upon the realization, devastated her and killed her very soul. It felt as if she lived hell on earth. *Yes, that's what I am going through,* she thought.

Mary felt a strong urge within her spirit that she needed to break this cycle and she needed deliverance and complete freedom from this torment. Mary pondered over these thoughts, and she heard Alex say, "The Spirit of God bids you to come. He said if He knocks, you must open the door unto Him, and He will come in and sup with you. Whosoever will call on the name of the Lord will be saved." These words pierced through her spirit. She felt that she had to reach out and grab this offer that the Lord was giving her. He spoke convincingly of the Lord and the simple, quiet strength that faith in Christ brings to a life.

She was surprised when she heard herself say out loud, "Lord Jesus!"

It felt as if she reached out with her hands outstretched towards Christ Jesus—just like Peter did, in desperation, when he began to drown in the waters. Peter called out to Jesus with an outstretched hand, "Lord Jesus, Save me."

Alex realized quickly that the Spirit of God had begun His work in her heart. There was conviction in her. He said, "If you confess with your mouth that Jesus is Lord and believe in your heart that God raised Him from the dead, you will be saved."

Yes, that's what I need, Mary thought.

Mary closed her eyes. She knew she needed this total forgiveness from her Creator. She knew she needed that redemption from her sin to be liberated and set free from this bondage that tormented her time and again. Mary opened her mouth and prayed, "Forgive me, Lord. Give me grace to overcome my deep sorrow. I want to drink from the fountain of living water that you so freely offer to us. Lord, save me from my sins, my guilt, my fear. Set me free from the chains that have bound me for so many years. Lord, I surrender to You today. Have mercy on me."

As she finished her prayer, tears streamed down her face, and she buried her face in the palm of her hands and poured out her heart to Jesus Christ. Pastor Alex knelt beside her, laid his hand on her shoulders, and prayed for her. He knew Mary was getting her deliverance, and the Lord was touching her very heart and soul, liberating her from all the bondage and heartbreak that she struggled with. The healing power of Christ flowed through her inmost being and healed her grief-stricken, guilt-ridden heart; the kind of healing that no man can give her but only the divine touch of Christ.

Both Alex and Mary experienced the divine presence of God right at the moment in that room.

Mary felt in her spirit that she was forgiven by her unborn child, Chloe, and the peace of God filled her heart. She knew that she was forgiven by God as well, and all her pain, agony, torment, and guilt was replaced by joy in her spirit. As she basked in this divine presence healing her soul, she knew that when it was time for her to meet Chloe, it would be a joyous one. The liberation that she felt at that moment was unexplainable. She continued to remain with her eyes closed, and her thoughts flew back to Chloe.

She came with the radiance of an angel, with a sweet smile and love in her eyes for her mother. Mary could hear her voice in her head. "Mother! God used my death to give you eternal life. I have forgiven you, mother. Even though I did not have an opportunity to live, God had a plan just as it is written in Psalm 139:15-16: 'When my bones were being formed, carefully put together in my mother's womb, when I was growing there in secret, you knew that I was there—you saw me before I was born. The days allotted to me had all been recorded in your book before any of them began.' God knew, mother. Again, in Genesis 50:20, 'You intended to harm me, but God intended it all for good. He brought me to this position so I could save the lives of many people.' Yes, mother, God used me, even though I wasn't born. He used me to bring you to Him. And now, you can share our story to encourage others not to make the same mistake that you did. In case they have, please tell them He can make all things new. God can make all things new, mother." Mary opened her eyes. Chloe's voice still echoed in her mind. She turned around and looked at Alex.

Alex understood now that the person he was seeing was a new creation, a new Mary with a mission.

Don't miss out!

Visit the website below and you can sign up to receive emails whenever C.Orville McLeish publishes a new book. There's no charge and no obligation.

https://books2read.com/r/B-A-GABRB-MSJVD

BOOKS 2 READ

Connecting independent readers to independent writers.

Did you love *Chloe: A Christian Novel*? Then you should read *FAITH: A Theological Memoir*[1] by C.Orville McLeish!

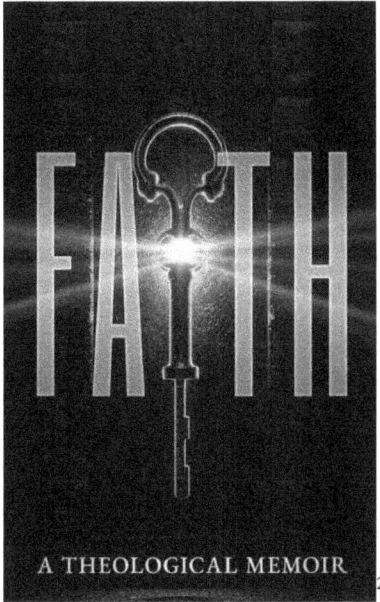

Author C. Orville McLeish hails from humble beginnings, yet his family's spirit was unbroken. Despite financial constraints that limited educational pursuits and the acquisition of certain earthly possessions and comfort, he discovered a "faith" that inevitably guided him through many life challenges and transformed him into a voice echoing God's ability to elevate a soul from obscurity to prominence. His was a journey of faith, overcoming hurdles, and challenging conventional perspectives. His transparency reveals personal battles with fear and anxiety

1. https://books2read.com/u/mg89x6

2. https://books2read.com/u/mg89x6

before embracing an identity rooted in the understanding that we are reflections of God's image and true heirs of the Most High.Just as ordinary individuals in biblical times triumphed, so can a son of this generation. This theological memoir is a compelling reminder that you, too, can break free from the shadows of obscurity and despair. By discovering your identity in Christ, irrespective of your family background, race or social status, you possess the ability to believe, achieve, and transcend any limitations. You need not be confined to a life of obscurity and anguish. With a foundational understanding of your identity in Christ, coupled with trust and faith, you have the power to overcome obstacles and become who God created you to be.Adam and Eve were created perfect in a perfect world. They were as God-conscious as a human being can get. Yet, they made a bad choice. Despite their fall, the clarity with which Adam and Eve, and Cain, who became a murderous vagabond, was able to speak with God is fascinating. That clarity seems to be missing today, even with those who claim to be "prophetic." Comparing then and now can prove rather burdensome when the answers are not readily available. We have embraced a culture of self-sufficiency that lacks faith to the point where we do not consult God before making decisions. This is a very sad reality because we have learned to do life, and even church, without God, while simultaneously attaching His name to what we do in a way to create some measure of validity.If this world is going to change, there must be a restoration of our capacity to walk in God and with God by faith. We must relearn our total dependency on Him to the point where we do nothing without first consulting Him. This is a lost culture in our day, but I believe a generation will arise as it was in the days of Seth when men begin to call on the name of the Lord again. Despite our modernization and self-aggrandizing culture, we can usher in an age where men once again put all their hope, trust and faith in God, our Creator and Abba. This is the clarion call on this generation and generations to come. Will you answer that call?May we, the ecclesia, rise in faith, trusting God with the same fervor and conviction as the saints of old, and may our lives be a living testament to His enduring faithfulness and grace.

Read more at https://clevelandomcleish.com/.

Also by C.Orville McLeish

Christian Youth Faith-Walkers Series
Detour: A Christian Novel
The Preacha And The Prostitute: A Christian Novel
Agents of Christ: The Prodigal Daughter: A Christian Novel
Chains: A Christian Novel
The Waiting Room: A Christian Novel
Chloe: A Christian Novel

Made in God's Image Series
The Path to Spiritual Enlightenment
You Are Born To Win

The Unshakable Series
FAITH: A Theological Memoir

Standalone

Girl Unknown

Who I Am In Christ Daily Devotionals

How to Receive Your Healing

Sons of God: A Study on the Biblical Narrative of the Sons of God

Made in God's Image: We are Partakers of God's Divine Nature

A Glorious Church: In Pursuit of the Biblical Model of Christianity

Watch for more at https://clevelandomcleish.com/.

About the Author

C. Orville McLeish is a successful entrepreneur, and an acclaimed multi-award-winning author, playwright, and screenwriter. He is a professional ghostwriter, copy editor and self-publishing service provider. With a deep commitment to intellectual and mystical theology, he intertwines his passion for health, fitness, longevity, and Christian spirituality. A proud graduate of Writer's Digest University and the School of Kingdom Mysteries, Cleveland is currently pursuing a master's in theological studies at Gordon-Conwell Theological Seminary.

Read more at https://clevelandomcleish.com/.

About the Publisher

Providing Writing and Self-Publishing Coaching, Consultation, and Services to New and Seasoned Authors since 2018.
    Read more at https://hcpbookpublishing.com/.

www.ingramcontent.com/pod-product-compliance
Lightning Source LLC
Chambersburg PA
CBHW032215040426
42449CB00005B/610

*9 7 8 1 9 5 8 4 0 4 9 4 2 *